AF278729

THE SIGN PAINTER'S GUIDE

OR HINTS AND HELPS TO SIGN PAINTING, GLASS GILDING, PEARL WORK, etc.

CONTAINING ALSO MANY VALUABLE RECEIPTS AND METHODS, AND MUCH GENERAL INFORMATION IN THE VARIOUS BRANCHES OF THE BUSINESS

JAMES T. GARDINER

Published by Left of Brain Books

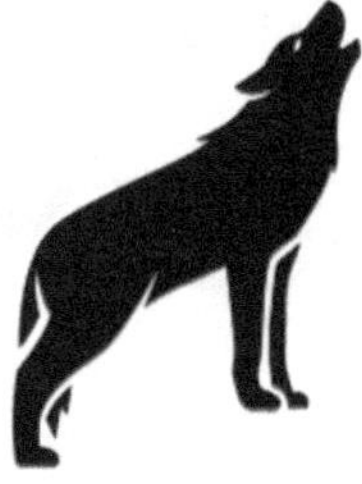

Copyright © 2021 Left of Brain Books

ISBN 978-1-396-31811-5

First Edition

All rights reserved. No part of this publication may be reproduced, distributed, or transmitted in any form or by any means, including photocopying, recording, or other electronic or mechanical methods, without the prior written permission of the publisher, except in the case of brief quotations embodied in critical reviews and certain other noncommercial uses permitted by copyright law. Left of Brain Books is a division of Left of Brain Onboarding Pty Ltd.

Table of Contents

INTRODUCTORY.

In answer to numerous inquiries and applications for information and instruction in Sign Painting and its Ornamental branches I have been induced to publish this little work, which I now offer to the trade, and to those interested in this beautiful art, confident that its reliability and accuracy will insure it a hearty welcome and recommendation from every Painter into whose hands it may come.

That the work is small is no detriment to its practical value. Many of the receipts and methods it contains are very valuable; the writer paid fifty dollars a few years ago for two of them, and many of the others could not be purchased at the present time for twice the price asked for this work.

Perfection is not claimed for this more than for any other work of the kind, but what is claimed for it is that it contains more real practical and valuable information to the Sign Painter than has ever before been presented to him in a published form.

Much of my time of late years has been occupied in giving instructions in the various departments of Sign Painting. For a course of such instructions I have received from $25 to $50, according to facilities offered. There are many who would, but, from various reasons, are unable to avail themselves of this mode of gaining knowledge. My object is to place before every one who may desire it, no matter where located, the same advantages at a much less cost.

Remember I do not profess to manufacture ready made Sign Painters. Much study and practice alone will accomplish that. But I do profess to be able to materially help those who are inclined to help themselves.

It is an old maxim, and none the less a true one, that, "What is worth doing at all, is worth doing well," and I would like in the outset to impress this important fact upon the mind of every aspirant to fame in this direction, "If you would be a Sign Painter, be a good one."

And your first step toward this accomplishment will be to secure a good master, or what is the same thing, the works of a good master as your guide.

There are several of these to be had, but McLee's Alphabets are now accepted and recognized by all as the most perfect in form and symmetry, and the best adapted in every respect to the requirements of modern Sign Painting.

As much practice is essentially and absolutely necessary to the formation of a perfect letter, the pupil consequently loses or spends unprofitably a great deal of his time in this way. This I have found to be a great drawback to progress, as gain is with most of us a great incentive to duty. I have, however, remedied this by the introduction of the Traceotype, or card-board letter, which, as well as affording excellent practice, enables the beginner to make his work pay him from the start. They comprise alphabets of all the modern styles of letters in use by Sign Painters, cut out of tar board in sizes varying from two to twelve inches or larger, when ordered. They are all ways convenient, and a Sign of any number of lines may be laid out, spaced, and the letters perfectly traced, ready for the brush in a few minutes time, when hours would be required to accomplish the same by the ordinary method.

They are being received with much favor by many of our expert Painters who speak very highly of their time and labor-saving qualities.

My thanks are due to those of my fellow craftsmen who have aided and encouraged me, and for the favorable opinions entertained by them of my efforts in the past to advance and improve the beautiful art to which I have been so long and so ardently attached.

J. T. G.

Rules for Making and Spacing Letters.

The letters most used by Sign Painters are Roman, Italic, round and square Block, half Block, or Egyptian, Lower Case and Script.

Roman is the general favorite with letterers. It is also the most difficult to make. Egyptian is the simplest and easiest made, and is therefore generally chosen by beginners.

Nine of the Roman letters, viz., B, D, E, G, O, P, Q, R and T, when properly made, will occupy one-eighth more in width than in height. Six letters, viz., C, F, J, L, S and Z, will occupy the same space from left to right as they do in height. Seven letters, viz., A, K, N, U, V, X and Y, one-sixteenth more in width than in height. H, one-fourth; M, one-third, and W, one-half more in width than height. I, two-thirds of its height in width, and occupies one-sixteenth less in width than in height.

The circular letters, C, G, O, Q and S, to appear equal in size with the rest, must be made to project a little above and below the line.

The upper part of B, E, F and R should occupy a trifle less space on the main line of each letter than the lower part, and the upper horizontal projecting curve of B and R should, in the same proportion, be a trifle the smallest. The connecting bar of H, and the center bar of E and F, should be a very little above the center of those letters. The perpendicular width of the curve for P should take up just half the length of the main limb of that letter. The bottom curve of J, with the projecting line on its top, should occupy the same space as the letters C or S. The upper curve of should be smaller than the lower curve. The tail of the R should be made full, and to project nearly as far as the upper curve. The last limb of G should terminate at a little less than half its height. The upper portion of the Y should join the main body of the letter at half its height, and the lower curve of C should project a trifle beyond the upper one.

The width of the main body of a Roman letter must be regulated by its size. For a six inch letter the main stroke should be one inch and a-half wide, the fine stroke, or hair line, one-fourth inch. For a letter one foot in height it should be three inches, and the hair stroke one-half inch wide. And in the same proportion for larger or smaller letters.

The upper point of A and the lower points of V and W should be of the same width as the fine, or hair line.

If two lines are drawn one inch apart, and divided into nine compartments one inch and one-eighth each, the letters B, D, E, G, O, P, Q, R and T will each fill a compartment; then divide off six compartments of one inch square for C, F, J, L, S and Z; then seven compartments of one inch and one-sixteenth each for A, K, N, U, V, X and Y, For H allow one inch and a quarter, for M one inch and three-eighths, for W one inch and a half. I will take a space five-eighths of an inch wide, while & will require one-sixteenth less than an inch in width.

LOWER CASE ROMAN.

This is a very popular letter with Sign Painters, and when properly formed, for grace and beauty, is only equalled by its near ally, the Roman Capitals.

The main body of thirteen letters, viz: A, B, D, G, H, K, N, P, Q, U, V, X and Y, will occupy a square each; letters C, E, O R, S, T and Z, require one-sixteenth less width than height; I and 1, one-half their height in width. These relative proportions are stated without their projecting limbs above and below the main body of the letter, which projection should be one half the height of the main body of the letter.

ITALIC CAPITALS.

These have all the forms and peculiarities of the Roman Capitals, slightly condensed, and at an angle of sixty-three degrees.

LOWER CASE ITALIC.

This letter is rarely introduced in sign painting, but is the prevailing style in show card writing, or wherever quick, off-hand lettering is required.

There is no regular rule governing these letters, if gracefully formed, a little crowding does not injure their appearance; there are many opportunities where they may be worked in advantageously and with good effect in sign work.

Block Letters.

This is the boldest and most massive of all the styles of letters, and is governed by the same rules and proportions in regard to height and breadth as the Roman Capitals; unlike that letter, however, it may be elongated or condensed to a very great extent without injury to its appearance.

The perpendicular and horizontal bars of this letter are the same in size throughout.

By dispensing with curves and using straight lines, and cutting the outside corners off diagonally, we have the Square Block, which is much better adapted to the purpose of elongation or enlargement than the round. The corners should be cut off to the extent of four fifths of the thickness of the main body of the letter; the inside corners may be either rounded or squared.

Next in order is the

Egyptian, or Half-Block.

These useful letters may be denominated the Painter's stand-by or substitute for all the letters, for when other styles fail for want of necessary space or other significant reasons, these will always be found to fill the bill exactly. When properly proportioned, they are inferior to none for beauty, but as substitutes they may be tortured and tormented with impunity into filling every conceivable space, but crowded and cramped as they often are, they fill every position assigned them with becoming dignity.

Their form and construction as well as their proportion, will be ascertained by drawing two parallel lines one inch apart, and two within these at three-sixteenths of an inch distance from the others for the horizontal bars of the letter. If five compartments of seven-eighths of an inch each are divided off, the letters **A, D, K, O,** and **Q,** will each fill a compartment, then divide off ten more three-fourths of an inch wide for **B, C, G, R, S, V, X, Y, Z,** and **&**; then three of five-sixteenths less than an inch in width, for **H, P,** and **U**; three of five-eighths wide for **E, N,** and **T, M** requires a space one-sixteenth less than one inch in width; **W,** a space one inch and one-eighth; **F, L,** and **J,** require a space, nine-sixteenths in width, and **I** a space three-sixteenths of its height in width.

Like the Block, this style of letter made either round or square. The body of the letter must invariably be of the same size all over.

The Traceotypes afford the best possible advantages for the study of all these letters, and will therefore be found a valuable adjunct to this work.

SCRIPT

This style of letter makes a beautiful sign but it is very difficult of execution. Some few sign writers make a speciality of it; but generally speaking, there is not enough of it done even in our large cities, to afford painters practice sufficient to attain any degree of perfection. Good penmanship is not essentially necessary in order to become a good Script writer. Some of our best are very inferior penmen. Writing on a sign-board is a very different process from writing on paper. It is necessary, however, to have a pretty correct idea of penmanship, and a good round text copy for your guide.

The "Line of Beauty," so termed by an eminent artist, is formed of two gentle curves, and that line occurs twenty-nine times in forming twenty Script Capitals; it is the first line *A*; the middle of *B*, *D*, *F*; last of *G*; fist part of *H*, *S*, *J*; two parts of *K*; part of *L*; three parts of *M*; two of *N*; part of *P*, *R*, *S*, *F*; two parts of *V*; four parts of *W*; last of *Y*; and middle of *Z*.

A little time judiciously devoted in examining this as a general principle—which is the most important part of twenty out of the twenty-six capital letters and by practice in making this one line gracefully will rapidly contribute to a correct formation of the capital letters. The letters in which the "Line of Beauty" is not introduced are *C*, *E*, *O*, *Q* and *X*.

In writing Capital Script, all the lines drawn towards the writer are to be gradually swelled and full lines, and all lines from the writer, are to be hair lines; and the curves of the capitals should be evenly true in their oval shape, and sloped to the same angle with the main body of the letter, that being 48 degrees.

The loop to be formed in making the first part of the letters *C* , *G* , *L* ; and *S* should be an equal curve on each side of the loop, which can easily be tested by drawing a straight line from the centre of its top curve to its union at the main body of the letter. If the curves and distances are not equal on both sides of the said straight line, they should be made so, to be correct and graceful.

The small or round text letters should be in the proportion of three-eighths of the size of the capitals, uniform angles and delicate hair lines being essential to their beauty and gracefulness.

SPACING.

There is no rule in Sign Painting to designate the exact distance between the letters forming a word or sentence. It is equally in bad taste, however, to crowd them too closely or to separate them too much.

In cities where painters are paid by the foot for lettering, many good jobs are spoiled by being spread too much, in order to measure a few feet more. This, I suppose, may be called one of the tricks of the trade. It is one, however, that does not reflect much credit on the workman.

The distance between letters must depend in a great measure upon the length of the word and the space it is to occupy. The following rules will be found to work well in regulating the spaces between Roman, Block or Egyptian Capitals. Take, for example, the word ABILITY. We will suppose the letters are each solid blocks of their own size, and six inches in height. We will also have a few blocks of one-quarter, and a few of one-half inch in thickness, to insert between the letters as we proceed.

By placing the letters A and B together we find that, in consequence of the pyramidical form of A, they are connected at the bottom, while there is a great deal of open space between them at the top, which seems to separate the letters sufficiently, but as they must not be connected anywhere we will be compelled to insert the smallest or one-quarter inch block between them.

The next letter is I, which must have a proportionate distance between it and B as between B and A. To accomplish this we will have to insert three of the one-half inch and one of the one-quarter inch blocks.

Between I and L it will be necessary, in order to keep up the same proportionate distance, to insert three one-half inch blocks; and in consequence of the large Open space caused by the projecting lower limb of L, the second I must only be separated from that letter by the smallest or one-quarter inch block.

T is next in order, and will be separated from I by three one-quarter inch blocks. The last letter, Y, when placed alongside of T, appears already sufficiently separated, but as the connection at the upper corner must be broken, we will again insert only the smallest or one-quarter inch block.

The word is now properly spaced, but may be extended at will by increasing the distance equally between each letter; or, suppose it is desirable to extend the word three inches, to do so it will be necessary to insert another one-half inch block between each of the letters.

Another method of spacing is to make the center of the letters the point from which to regulate the distances between them. For this we must draw a center line, that is, a line parallel with and at equal distance from the extreme outside lines.

Between all letters having crossbars at the top and bottom the distance must be the same, as in HID, but if another letter of the same kind follows, as HIDD, the distance will have to be reduced two-fifths, on account of the absence of the upper and lower bar on that side of D. With the next letter following, HIDDE, the same distance will be repeated, while the last letter, N, in HIDDEN, will be one fifth nearer still to the extreme limits of E, to counterbalance the open space formed by the projecting upper and lower limbs of that letter.

These rules will be of great service to the beginner, but to the practiced eye all rules are superfluous. It detects at a glance every imperfection; untiring perseverance is indispensable to the attainment of it, but all who desire it can and may possess it.

WALL LETTERING.

There are places and occasions, however, where even the critical eye of the expert will be somewhat at a loss. On the high blank walls which are, in our larger cities, often appropriated to signs, sometimes from fifty to one hundred feet in length, or more, and when an ordinary staging will not reach more than one-fourth that distance, the eye, in such close proximity, can take in but a very small proportion of the work to be done.

It is necessary in such cases to adopt some mode of laying out the work correctly, without going over it twice, as is ordinarily the case, saving thereby much time and labor in moving and adjusting staging, etc.

In doing similar work I have adopted the following rule, and have invariably found it a good one, and would therefore recommend it to all wall letterers:

Take the dimensions of the sign or space to be occupied by the sign, its length, width, and the number of lines into which it is to be divided. Mark off a similar space on paper on a scale of one inch to the feet, then lay out your lettering as you wish it to appear on the wall. When the sketch is complete, with your dividers and rule you can readily find the real dimensions of the letters, spaces, etc., marking them off as you go, in their respective places, in feet and inches.

If the sign is very large this sometimes necessitates several sheets of paper, but a reduced copy may be made for reference when at work, care being taken to preserve the measurements correct.

With this sketch and table of measurements you have the whole thing, as it were, in a nutshell. You may begin at either end of the work, carry along any number of lines, and by adhering strictly to your chart can not possibly commit an error.

For work of this kind the letterer will find a small pocket plumb line of great service in preserving the perpendicular form of the letter, which is sometimes very difficult to do when they are very large.

To Lay Out a Sign Correctly.

Much of the beauty of a Sign depends upon the variety of the letters introduced, and their arrangement into lines.

A very inferior job of lettering if well arranged will look infinitely better than a good job poorly arranged.

As a general thing a repetition of the same letter on two succeeding lines should be avoided. Nor should two lines following each other be precisely of the same length. When a sign is composed of a great many lines, curved or scroll lines may be used to advantage, but they should be thrown in gracefully and sparingly, or instead of beautifying they will mar the general design.

For a sign of but one line any style of letter may be used, always allowing an ample margin of at least two and a half or three inches around the board. Without this no sign will look well.

For a sign of two lines, the upper one in Roman and the lower in round or square Block, would be in good taste, being careful not to crowd the lines too closely, allowing about the same room between them as in the margin. When the lines are numerous it is customary to lay out the upper one in the form of a half circle, arranging the rest into half, three-quarter and full lines, with an occasional curve or scroll line.

When the line consists of but one word, as, for instance, AND, or the capital, & the space allowed must not be more than one-half what it is between the other lines, or the matter will appear too open or scattered.

The size of the letters used must depend upon the importance attached to the various words and sentences. Lines to which special prominence is to be given should always be in capitals as large as the number of letters and the space they are to occupy will admit. Lines of medium importance, in Egyptian or lower case. Avoid profuse flourishing; it often detracts from good work. Flourishes, if there are any, should be few, and very gracefully put in.

Chalk crayons should be used for laying out letters. The outlines may be traced previous to painting with black crayon or black lead pencil, and the chalk marks erased, or they will offer an obstruction to the free passage of the sable or camel hair brush over the surface.

COLORING AND SHADING.

There is scarcely any limit in the variety of colors that may be used in Sign Painting. Much, however, depends upon making a proper selection. That they are too often put on with an utter disregard of all the rules of harmony and good taste none will dispute.

Black and white are the most common of all colors, if colors they may be called. Some, I believe, pretend to dispute that fact. I shall not attempt to argue it here. To all intents and purposes they are colors, and very important ones.

A black letter on a white ground, and a white letter on a black ground, are perhaps as often introduced as any other. For both, a white ground work is necessary, the difference being that while in the former the black letter is painted on the surface of the white, in the latter the letter is marked out, then traced around, or is what the Sign Painter calls out in, and the ground work filled in with black. By this mode a much whiter letter is obtained than would be were the white letter painted upon a black surface, even if two coats were applied.

Cutting in has, for this reason, been very generally adopted by modern Sign Painters, in all cases where the color of the letter is lighter than the ground work. To the uninitiated it may appear somewhat of a back handed process, but after sufficient practice it becomes the preferable, and also the most speedy mode of work.

Green, blue, vermillion, Indian red and black are the colors principally used for cutting in.

The color of the letter or ground work of the sign previous to being cut in may be of white or of any desired tint. An imitation gold color is a very popular tint, and may be used in connection with any of the aforementioned colors with good effect.

When two or more colors are used in forming the body of a letter it is called a variegated letter.

A very pretty letter of this kind is made by using three different shades of the same color; for instance, divide the letter into three parts, fill in the upper part a bright green, the middle with a green a few shades darker, the lower part with darker still, or black.

Or, the upper part vermillion, the middle Indian red lightened a little with vermillion, and the lower part black. These three shades may be worked in many fanciful forms beside the above. They must not be blended together, but each color must be dry enough not to rub up when the other is put on.

These letters look best on a white or light ground, and require to be shaded.

For shading black letters on a white ground any light tint of blue, green or buff color may be used. The most prevalent is a light lead or pearl gray. (See Compounding of Colors.) The depth of shade, and also whether on the right or left of the letter, is optional. One-fifth of the height of the letter is a fair proportion, but may be much heavier. There should be a space between the shade and letter in the proportion of one-quarter inch to a six inch, and one-half inch to a twelve inch letter.

In a circular letter the shade should begin at a point one-twentieth of its height from the top, and extend around six-tenths of its entire circumference. In the other shades care should be taken to preserve a uniform angle.

A good effect is produced by introducing the line shade in connection with the ordinary shade; that is, a line following the entire inner edge of the shade at the distance from the letter already indicated. This line must be several shades darker than the shade tint. Or, if the shade tint is green, blue or pink, the line must be darker green, darker blue, and red. If lead, or pearl gray, the line must be a darker shade of the same color.

When more showy and expensive work is wanted another line may be added, with the color modified to a degree between that of the first line and the shade tint. This makes a very beautiful shade, and is only excelled by the blended shade, of which we shall soon have occasion to speak.

The width of the lines must be regulated by the size of the letter. For a twelve-inch letter about five-eighths of an inch; for a six-inch letter about three-eighths.

For cut-in signs, or where the ground is darker than the letter, the shade must be four or five degrees darker than the ground. The line shade may be used here also with equally good effect, the darkest or black line, nearest the letter, and gradually lightening down to the shade tint, or first color.

As black has no darker color, letters on black grounds are shaded with bright colors, either of one color, in lines, or with the blended shade. This is the most difficult to execute of all the shades, and consists of a combination of colors and tints worked in and blended together with most pleasing effect.

The lighter and bright tints form the side shades, the deeper color the lower, or under shade. This shade differs somewhat from the other shades we have described, in that it connects with the letter, no space being left between, as with the others.

The prevailing colors for blended shades are green, blue, red and yellow.

For green we begin at the extreme upper corner of the letter, with white, or a very pale tint of green, gradually deepening into an emerald green, and still deepening by mixture with chrome green until of that color. This is deep enough for the side shade. For the lower shade begin with light chrome green and finish with the deepest.

The colors used are white, emerald green and two shades of chrome green.

For blue begin with white or very pale blue tint, deepening gradually to a sky blue, and three or four shades deeper still for side shade. For lower shade begin with sky blue, and work off with deep ultramarine.

Ultramarine and white are all the colors necessary for this shade.

Red, or Carmine Shade—For side begin with very light pink, made with carmine and white, increasing its depth gradually with vermillion, and lightening the vermillion with carmine. For lower shade begin with vermillion and finish with carmine.

Colors used are white, vermillion and carmine.

Yellow Shade—Begin with white, blending and deepening with orange chrome until of that color. Darken slightly with raw sienna for side shade. For lower shade begin with a mixture of chrome yellow and raw sienna, finishing with burnt sienna.

White, orange chrome, raw sienna and burnt sienna are the colors used.

The thorough blending of the colors as you proceed is indispensable. To facilitate this good boiled linseed oil alone should be used for mixing the colors. If too much drier is added they will set too quick to allow the requisite blending.

The brushes used should be shorter haired than are required for lettering. There should be one for each tint, and two for blending purposes.

We will have to speak further on this shade in connection with gold lettering.

A very novel and attractive style of shading for large signs of one line is effected by lettering the sign twice—first with the shade tint, and afterward with the lettering color. The last letters must be two or three inches above the level of the first, and a corresponding distance to the right or left to give the proper effect.

Another method is to letter with the shade tint on an angle of sixty-three degrees, and afterward with the lettering color reversing the angle.

COMPOUNDING OF COLORS.

Light Gray is made by mixing white lead with lampblack, using more or less of each material as you wish to obtain a lighter or darker shade.

Buff is made from yellow ochre and white lead.

Silver or Pearl Gray—Mix white lead, Prussian blue, and a very slight portion of black.

Flaxen Gray is obtained by a mixture of white lead and Prussian blue, with a small addition of lake.

Oak Ground Color—Three parts white lead, one part yellow ochre, tinged slightly with Venetian red. This makes a good imitation Gold Color, much used for lettering. It may be made much richer and brighter by substituting chrome yellow for ochre.

Walnut Ground Color—Two-thirds white lead, one third Venetian red, yellow ochre and burnt umber; the proportion of the latter being determined by the desired tint.

Orange Color—Vermilion and chrome yellow.

Violet Color—Vermilion, mixed with Prussian blue and a small portion of white.

Purple—Indian red mixed with violet color.

Carnation—Lake and white.

Another Gold Color—Massicot or Naples yellow, with a small quantity of realgar and a very little white.

Olive Color may be obtained by black and blue, mixed with yellow.

Lead Color—Prussian blue and white, with a very little black.

Chestnut Color—Venetian red, yellow ochre and black. To make it lighter increase the quantity of yellow ochre.

Flesh Color—Lake, white lead and vermillion.

Light Willow Green—White, mixed with verdigris or emerald green.

Stone Color—White lead, yellow ochre, small quantities of Venetian red and black.

Fawn Color—White lead, yellow ochre and vermilion.

Chocolate Color—Lampblack and Spanish brown.

Portland Stone Color—Umber, white lead and yellow ochre. All these colors may be regulated by adding more or less of the light or dark ingredients.

Pure boiled linseed oil is the best under all circumstances for mixing colors for all the purposes of Sign Painting, except in cases of which we shall hereafter have to speak, where flat or turpentine color must be used.

Japan drier may be used with the oil, for drying purposes only, in such quantity as the necessity and urgency of the case demands.

Where boiled oil can not be obtained, raw oil, with a larger proportion of drier, may be substituted, but is not so good.

FLOCKING AND SMALTING.

Flock and smalt are now very generally used for the ground-work of gilded and cut-in signs. Flock consists of the dressings of woolen cloths, in the form of a fine powder. It may be had in a variety of colors, some of which are very beautiful; the principal are blue, green, scarlet, crimson and black. With the exception of the black these colors all fade when long exposed to the sun; they are, therefore, only used for inside work.

They may be used in connection with all the cutting-in colors we have before described. When a sign is intended to be flocked the ground color must be mixed with boiled oil alone. If too much drier is added it is liable to dry too fast, and the flock will not stick.

When the sign has been cut in and the ground filled up, and while the color is still wet, lay it down flat, with the face up, and with a fine sieve sift the flock upon it until it is entirely covered. It may then be turned partially over, to allow the surplus flock to fall off and be gathered up. When dry the letters may be brushed off lightly with a very soft brush or duster.

When a shade is necessary it must be put on with black previous to flocking, and while the ground color is still wet, and it will show very distinctly through the flock. In this way many fancy designs and ornaments may be worked in on the body of the sign that will look very beautiful through the rich colored flocks.

Letters on black flock grounds are seldom shaded when they are the blended shade is generally chosen. It must be allowed to dry thoroughly, so that the letter and shade may be cut in at the same time.

It may be necessary to mention here that where fancy colored flocks are used, the color of the cutting-in color should match as nearly as possible the color of the flock.

Smalts are more durable, and their colors, though not so bright or showy as those of flock, are more permanent; they are, therefore, better adapted for outside signs. The principal colors are blue, green, vermilion, Indian red or brown, purple and black. (See receipt for making smalts.)

The process of flocking and smalting are the same, with the exception of the dark shade. In flocking it is put on before the flock; in smalting afterward, and when the smalt is dry, as the black is not seen as distinctly through the smalt as through the flock.

COATING SIGN BOARDS.

This is too important an item in connection with Sign Painting for us to overlook, and a few hints in regard to it will not be out of place here. Much time lost, and valuable work ruined, is the result of improperly coated sign boards; or, in other words, boards that have been prepared in a hurry, receiving in some cases two or three coats in a day. To this cause is attributable the blistering and peeling, and other defects which their surface exhibits when exposed a short time to the weather and the rays of the sun. In the first place we would say, always allow one coat to dry thoroughly before putting another on. This is the chief consideration.

For painted signs, the board, when ready for lettering, should present a glossy surface. This is effected in the following manner: Before any paint is put on, the board should be well examined, and the knots and gum spots covered with shellac, to prevent their showing through. While this is drying mix a little white lead with pure boiled oil, rather thin, and give it a coat. This should have at least twenty-four hours to dry. It may then be rubbed lightly with fine sand paper, and the knots and uneven parts filled with white lead putty. In four hours it may receive the second coat, for which take lead as before and mix with three parts turpentine to one of boiled oil, to which a little dryer may be added. This coat may be made something near the color it is intended to have the sign. It should now stand fifteen hours, when it will, after a slight rub with very fine sandpaper, be ready for the third and last coat. This may be of any color desired, and mixed with boiled oil, adding only a very little drier. This in twenty-four hours will be hard and dry, and will present the proper surface for lettering.

For Gold Signs the surface should present a half or eggshell gloss. To effect this follow the directions we have just given for the first and second coats. The third or last must be of lead, mixed one-third oil and two-thirds turpentine, with a small portion of drier. It is customary in this case to make the last coat of a light lead color, in order that the chalk marks may be more readily seen.

There is still another method of preparing a sign—one that is adopted when a varnished or polished surface is intended, and for which four or five coats is often necessary to secure a proper degree of smoothness. Follow the rules already laid down for the first and second coats; for the third mix with three parts turpentine and one part hard drying coach varnish; a little more turpentine may be added for the fourth coat, while the fifth should be a good heavy coat of color and varnish alone. When dry it should be rubbed down to an eggshell gloss with ground pumice stone and water, on a piece of woolen cloth. It will then be ready for lettering or ornamenting, after which it should be well varnished with coach-body varnish. It is necessary to add that all colors used for lettering and ornamenting on grounds prepared in this manner, with the exception of gold size, should be mixed in the same way, that is, three parts turpentine to one part varnish and drier.

SIZING AND GILDING.

There are four varieties or shades of gold leaf, viz., light, medium, deep and extra deep. The former is used principally for car and omnibus lettering and ornamenting, or wherever a large amount of scroll work is done, its lightness showing to better advantage the brilliant transparent colors used in shading.

For sign work the deep and extra deep only are used. There are many imitations of gold leaf, some of which are very good, but of no utility whatever in Sign Painting, as they turn black immediately on exposure. They are much used by japanners and other ornamenters, whose work requires to be heavily varnished.

We will now take a board prepared in the manner described for a gold sign, and proceed to lay it out, preparatory to sizing. For this we will use chalk, the leadish tint of the color enabling us to see the white chalk marks very distinctly. Prepared chalk or crayon is the best, the common being apt to scratch the surface, which will show very plainly through the gold. After the letters or design has been made with chalk, the outlines should be retraced with a soft lead pencil, and the chalk marks erased. It will then be ready for sizing.

Gold size is a preparation of fat oil, or boiled linseed oil that has become fat from heat and exposure; with this is ground very finely a little yellow ochre or chrome yellow. It is thinned to a proper consistency with venus or fat turpentine, and a small quantity of liquid drier added. It is then applied with a brush, in the same manner as paint, to the letters or part intended to be gilt. In ten or twelve hours, on applying the finger, it will be found to be dry, but having a slight tack or stickiness, without adhering to the finger in the least. This is sufficient to hold the gold leaf which may be now laid on. Good size should retain this tack for at least forty-eight hours.

Where the letters or sized part is large enough to take a full leaf in width it may be laid on out of the book, in the following manner. Open the book of leaf, allowing the gold to remain on the right-hand side; turn it over carefully between the thumb and forefinger of each hand, face forward, until it is adjusted in its proper position on the letter, when the paper may be slightly pressed with the backs of the fingers of the right hand, leaving the gold in its place; then open to the next leaf and proceed in the same manner, carefully fitting each leaf together, leaving no space between them uncovered; after all is covered that will admit of full leaves being laid, for the remainder we will use the gilder's knife, tip and cushion. Some little practice will be found necessary to the skillful handling of these articles. We will now empty about a half a book upon the cushion, which is done by slightly blowing each leaf as you turn to it out of the book into the cushion. Now with the point of the knife carefully take one leaf from among the rest, lay it on the front part of the cushion, getting it in such a position that a slight breath will open it to its full size, and spread it out flat; out it across with the knife as often as is necessary to reduce it to the size required; draw the tip once or twice across your hair or over the surface of a tallow candle—a slight greasy moisture is necessary to cause the gold to adhere to it; now lift a piece of gold upon the points of the tip and lay it gently in its place on the sign or sized part, and proceed in this way until every opening is covered; then with a bunch of fine cotton wool pounce the gilded part lightly, and rub down until every edge and joint disappears, and until the gold has received quite a high polish.

The letters may now be shaded with the blended shade, and when dry out in and flocked or smalted black; or they may be cut in and flocked or smalted black without any shade; or they may be flocked or smalted in any color desired; or they may be cut in and shaded without flock or smalt, in all cases being guided by the rules already laid down.

When a gold sign is to be finished with a varnished surface the process is somewhat different. We will illustrate it by taking a board already prepared with the varnish ground, and reduced to an eggshell gloss, in the manner already described. It is now ready for laying out and sizing, previous to which it should be pounced lightly with a cloth, in which a little fine whiting has been tied up, to prevent any gold from adhering to the varnish.

We will not use the oil size for this sign, but instead a size composed of four-fifths coach varnish and one-fifth fat oil, into which, as before, a little yellow has been finely ground. We will use turpentine to reduce it to a paper consistency for the brush.

Size the letters very carefully, keeping the edges and corners straight and square. When it has dried to the requisite tack, gild and polish as before. It is now ready for shading, and the shade should in this case be brought into contact with the gold, in order to straighten any unevenness along the edge. The plain or line shade may be adopted, whichever is desired. The high lights are all that is necessary now to complete the letter, that is, a fine yellow or straw colored line on the edge opposite to the shade, which, besides adding very much to the appearance of the letter, is very useful in straightening up any unevenness along the edge. When this is dry the surface of the sign should be wiped off with a damp sponge, to remove any whiting that may remain, after which it is ready for varnishing.

SHADING GOLD DESIGNS, SCROLLS, etc.

Gold devices and designs are so often introduced in Sign Painting that it is highly important to know what forms the best shade for such designs. Asphaltum varnish is more used fen this purpose perhaps, than anything else, and it seems to answer very well. It is nearer to the natural shade of gold than any other color known. Its chief recommendation, however, is that it can be used quick, drying in a few minutes. Coat after coat may be applied until the darkest shade is attained, and the work in a very short time completed. It is objected to as not being durable, but if well varnished it is quite as durable as any other color that is used for the same purpose.

Another shading color for gold is made from raw and burnt sienna and lake, adding of each until the required shade is obtained.

In car and omnibus painting transparent colors are often used with beautiful effect in shading gold ornaments. The colors used for this purpose are verdigris green, ultramarine blue, carmine, scarlet, and crimson lake.

In shading gold begin with the lightest shade; reduce the asphaltum to the proper consistency by dipping the brush in turpentine and working it until of the required tint. When this is dry lay on the next darker shade, and so on until the darkest shade is attained. In all cases this work should be varnished well, or it will not bear exposure.

GILDING ON GLASS.

In no department of Sign Painting has so much progress and improvement been made, or such a degree of perfection been attained, as this; in no other has such a general interest been manifested; and the demand for this beautiful work has grown to such an extent that it is essentially necessary, for successful competition, that every painter should thoroughly understand it. Having devoted much of our time to the study and practice of this class of work, we will proceed to lay before our readers such facts and information relating to it as our own and the experience of other first class workmen has suggested.

We would remark in the first place, that the better the quality of the glass the better will be the appearance of the work. Although we can not always be choosers in this respect, yet whenever we can we will always, for gilding purposes, prefer the single or double French, the crystal, or English or French plate. These qualities are clearer and freer from imperfections than any other. Pittsburgh glass may sometimes be found tolerably clear, but it generally imparts to the gold a bluish tint; it has also very often a smoky surface, which no amount of cleaning will remove. This is also highly prejudicial to both gilding and coloring, destroying the effect of both.

Having selected our glass, we next proceed to clean and prepare it for gilding. For this purpose take equal parts nitric and acetic acid in the proportion of one ounce of each to a half pint of water. Go over the surface of the glass with this, allowing it to remain a few moments, then clean the glass in the ordinary way, using soft water and whiting. When the whiting is dry wipe it off clean, and polish well with chamois or buckskin. Especial care must be taken to remove every particle of whiting from the surface.

Our next step is to prepare a pattern for our work. For this take a sheet of paper the size required, and draw upon it correctly the design intended for the glass. The lines in the drawing must be traced upon both sides of the paper, which may be done by using the magic tracing paper, or by holding the drawing against a window pane, and tracing the lines as they are reflected through by the light.

We will now adjust the pattern in its proper position on the front of the glass, securing it in its place with a little mucilage or paste at intervals around the margin. When this is dry it may be set upon the easel, or in a flat position, with the pattern on the underside. It will then be ready for gilding.

The size must now be prepared, and for this it is necessary to have distilled, or filtered soft water. It is absolutely essential to good work that the water used shall be soft and pure. Take shred, or Russian isinglass, and to a pint of water add a piece about the size of the smallest finger nail. The water should be hot enough to thoroughly melt the isinglass, but must not be allowed to boil.

The size may now be tested by spreading a little with the brush on a very clean piece of glass, and laying a part of a leaf of gold upon it. If this, when dry, will not allow of being rubbed quite hard with fine cotton wool without injury to the gold, the size is not strong enough, and more isinglass must be added. To find out when it is too strong, take a pointed cedar or pine stick, and with it draw a line through the gold. If the line is clean and well defined the size is right; if jagged, uneven, or rough it is too strong and more water must be added. The size must not be used too hot or too cold; a little less than lukewarm will be found to work best. The best brush for laying size on glass is a flat camel hair varnish brush not more than two inches wide.

Having reduced our size to a proper consistency we proceed to lay the leaf, being guided in this by the lines of the drawing seen through the glass.

Before commencing empty half the contents of a book of gold upon the cushion; with the knife, as before, bring one leaf forward and spread it out; now wet a portion of the glass with the size, and lay on as large a piece of the gold as you can conveniently lift with the tip; wet the glass again and lay on the next piece, proceeding in the same manner until the design, or the part to be gilded, is entirely covered. It should then be allowed to dry thoroughly, after which it may be rubbed lightly with very fine cotton wool. The cracks and openings, and other imperfections, should now be patched, cutting the leaf to the required size, and sizing and laying it on as before. In patching up the brush should be worked with very little size in it, or the gold is liable to be washed off.

When the patching is completed, and it has again become dry, the loose gold may be wiped off with the cotton, and it is ready for washing. This may be done with the sizing brush, but a wider one of the same kind is better. Hold the glass perpendicular on its edge, dip the brush in the size, draw it quickly across the gold, repeating it until the whole surface has been washed. When dry it may be burnished with the cotton wool. If the gold is not now sufficiently clear and brilliant the washing and burnishing process should be repeated until it has become so; but the second washing will generally be found sufficient. The glass should in all cases be set upon its edge to dry.

The pattern may be removed from the glass previous to the washing and burnishing process. It should be cut away from the pasted parts, leaving them adhering to the glass in such a manner that it may at any time be easily replaced in its former position.

The face of the design, or drawing, is now rubbed over with a little dry chrome yellow or whiting, very little being allowed to remain on the surface. It is now placed upon the back, or gilded side of the glass, in the precise position it occupied when on the other side. This will easily be accomplished by the aid of the pieces of the pattern paper still adhering to the front of the glass, and which must fit exactly opposite to the parts from which they were separated. When secured in this position by a little paste as before, the next step will be to trace carefully with a hard lead pencil all the outlines of the drawing, which will, by reason of the color that has been rubbed on the other side of the paper, be transferred to the surface of the gold, upon which, after removing the pattern, a very distinct impression will be found.

It is now ready for the backing color, for which mix a little prepared lamp black with equal parts of japan and copal varnish, thinning with turpentine to a proper working consistency. With this and a fine sable or camel hair pencil trace the outlines of the design upon the gold, filling in the solid parts afterward with a large brush.

After standing eight or ten hours the superfluous gold may be washed off, using for this purpose a very fine piece of sponge, or cotton wool, slightly wet. Great care must be exercised in order that the fine, or hair lines, may not be disturbed. When thoroughly clean it is ready for coloring and shading.

Asphaltum varnish mixed with a little of the prepared lamp black makes a very good and convenient backing for gold where a quick job is desired. It is more liable, however, to be rubbed up in cleaning, and is not as durable.

When many copies of the same design is to be made it is necessary, in order to facilitate work, to have a pricked pattern, the lined pattern being used only as a guide in laying the gold. After this is done, with a pounce bag and the pricked pattern, any number of duplicates of the drawing may be transferred to the surface of the gold in a few moments, ready for the backing up process.

It is not necessary, in this case, to paste the pattern to the glass. It should be made large enough to fold a little under the glass on two sides, the weight of the glass retaining it in its proper position.

When the style of shade has been decided on it should be laid out on the face of the glass with a French chalk or soapstone pencil, to be had for the purpose. The mode of shading depends, in a great measure, upon the color it is intended to have for the body or ground work of the glass; for instance, if a blended shade and a blue, green, brown, or any dark background is desired, the background should be put on first, carefully cutting around and leaving the shade open. As soon as the ground is dry the blended shade may be put on, differing only in this respect from the blended shade before described, in that the colors are not seen on the side on which they are worked, but on the reverse side, making a thorough blending of each color essential to the beauty of the work.

When either a plain or a line shade is desired it is put on previous to the background.

Where a blended shade and no background is required, a heavy line shade of black must first be laid out and painted outside of the blended shade. This, in the capacity of a double shade, adds much to the appearance of the latter, and is of material assistance in the blending process.

A method much adopted, and which, it is claimed secures greater durability for the work, is to outline the letters first with imitation gold color, and afterward gild. The line protects the gold during those seasons when the inside and outside temperature keeps the glass in a sweaty condition, and which would otherwise be apt to find its way under the surface of the gold to the ultimate destruction of the work.

As good a job, however, can not be made in this way, the line being detrimental to the proper washing and burnishing of the gold. And as all exposed work should, on completion, receive a coat of wearing body varnish, covering the edges securely, thus rendering them almost indestructible the utility of the outlining process disappears entirely.

The interior of gold letters on glass are capable of being richly colored and ornamented in a variety of ways. Openings of various forms and sizes corresponding with the shape of the letter are made, in some of them the gold merely forming an outline. These openings are first shaded, and then filled in with appropriate tints or colors. The most beautiful of all ornamentation of this kind being known as

PEARL WORK.

This process consists in covering the openings in the interior of the letters, with a very thin shell of pearl, prepared for the purpose, in the following manner: Take a clean camel hair brush and a little very clear demar varnish and varnish the openings of two or three letters, running it a little over on the letter all around. On the top of the varnish proceed carefully to lay the pearl, breaking it to the proper size and fitting it together as closely as possible until the opening is covered; proceed in like manner with the and next until all are covered. When the varnish is dry the pearl will be firmly attached to it. Now mix a little silver, or pearl gray color and coat over the pearl covering all the openings. This completes the work.

IMITATION PEARL.

A good imitation of pearl for patent medicine, and other advertising signs where cheapness is the great desideratum is made by using copper foil instead of pearl, in the following manner: Coat the openings in the letters with silver or pearl gray color mixed with demar varnish. It must be put on thin and transparent. When this is dry take the copper foil and crumble it as much as possible between the fingers. Cut it to the size and lay over the letters, the white side down. A little varnish may be used to make it adhere; but the back will secure it sufficiently in its place without anything else. Dead, or Etruscan gold, is often introduced in ornamenting the interiors of letters. This is effected by sizing the opening with varnish or oil size, and gilding according to that process. The varnish or oil imparts to it an appearance of dead, or unfurnished gold.

ETCHING AND SCRATCHING.

Beautiful and elaborate figures and designs are wrought in gold in the following manner: Gild and burnish a sufficient portion of the glass to fully cover the design. Transfer the ornament to the gold, using either the traced or pricked pattern. Lay it upon a dark surface; with the point of a hard wood stick trace all the outlines through the gold; cut down the bristles of two small sized flat fitches to one-third of their usual length. One should be smaller than the other. With these shade the drawing, brushing out the gold entirely where the drawing is black, and blending it off gradually into the lighter parts; in short, make a correct and finished drawing upon the gold. The dark surface underneath will assist by giving it the appearance of a pencil drawing. When complete it may be backed up, and as soon as dry the surplus gold washed off.

In doing this work it is necessary to have about four fitches, prepared as above, in size from one-fourth to one inch; several hard and soft wood sticks of various sized points, round and square; a few scratching tools, or needles, tied together for that purpose, from two to twelve forming a set. With these, and what is more indispensable, a good knowledge of drawing, any work of this kind may be easily accomplished.

LAYING SILVER LEAF.

Silver leaf is now used to a very great extent; for lettering and ornamenting on glass. It must be treated in every respect as gold leaf.

ENGRAVING AND ORNAMENTING GLASS
WITH ACID.

Although this beautiful art cannot, strictly speaking, be considered a branch of the Sign Painting business, it is in many respects so nearly allied to it, that a thorough knowledge of it cannot but be beneficial to every Sign Painter.

It consists of cutting or engraving letters or other ornaments on plain, ground and colored glass, for use in churches, offices, doors, vestibules, lamps, &c., by a process which differs somewhat from the usual mode of grinding, by which the same work can be done at a much reduced price.

There are two articles indispensable in this work: fluoric (sometimes called hydro-fluoric) acid, and the etching or protective varnish. The former, on being applied, eats its way into the surface of the glass; the latter is used to confine the acid to the limits within which it is to act.

Of colored glass, there are two kinds; one is colored entirely through the glass, the other, only on one side. The latter only, is suitable for engraving purposes.

To describe the process more fully, take a sheet of colored glass, of the size required for a lamp or transparency, make a pattern of your letters or design, prick it, and with the pounce bag transfer it upon the colored side of the glass; this can be told by holding the edge of the glass towards you, or by chipping off a small splinter. The small white dots made by pouncing the pattern will show quite distinctly on the dark surface of the glass.

Now cut in the letters carefully with the protective varnish, afterwards filling up with the same the entire groundwork of the glass. When this is dry, take pitch, prepared for the purpose, or shoemakers' wax, and form a border or edge around the glass; pour on the acid until the letters or parts upon which it is to act are entirely submerged; let it remain until it has eaten through the colored surface into the clear glass, then pour off the acid and wash well with water. After removing the varnish the letters will be perfectly clear, while the balance of the glass, protected by the varnish, is of the original color.

Letters etc., may be formed on ground glass, in the same manner as on stained or colored, the letters being cut in and the rest of the surface being filled up with the varnish as before; the acid will dissolve the ground surface, leaving it perfectly transparent so that when the varnish is removed the letters are quite clear, while the rest of the surface is ground.

The following method for grinding glass will be found useful. After you have cut or engraved a name or other design upon uncolored glass and wish it to show off to better advantage by permitting the light to pass only through the letters, you can do so by taking a piece of flat brass sufficiently large not to dip into the letters, but pass over them when gliding upon the surface of the glass; then with flour of emery, and keeping it wet, you can grind the whole surface very quickly, the letters having been eaten below the general surface, remaining perfectly clear.

Where a large quantity of glass is to be ornamented with the same design, stencil plates are used, by which the varnish is applied on those parts of the glass to be protected against the action of the acid. In this manner the large ornamental glass plates often used in offices, doors, &c., are produced at a moderate price, which would be impossible if the figures were all drawn in detail by hand labor.

ETCHING ON GLASS.

Druggist's bottles, bar tumblers, signs, and glassware of every description can be lettered in beautiful style of art by simply giving the article to be engraved or etched a thin coat of etching varnish, and the application of fluoric acid. Before doing so, the glass must be thoroughly cleaned, and heated so that it can hardly be held. The varnish is then to be applied lightly over, and made smooth by dabbing it with a small ball of silk, filled with cotton. When dry and even, the lines may be traced on it by a sharp steel instrument cutting clear, through the varnish to the glass. The varnish must be removed clean from each letter otherwise it will be an imperfect job. When all is ready pour on or apply with a feather the fluoric acid, filling each letter. Let it remain until it etches to the required depth, then wash off the water and remove the varnish.

FLUORIC ACID FOR ETCHING AND ENGRAVING ON GLASS.

You can make your own fluoric acid by getting the fluor or Derbyshire spar, pulverizing it, and putting all of it into sulphuric acid, which the acid will cut or dissolve. Inasmuch as fluoric acid is destructive to glass, it cannot be kept in common bottles, but must be kept in lead or gutta-percha bottles.

The protective varnish is made of equal parts of parafine or virgin wax and asphaltum; mix hot and thin with turpentine.

ETCHING VARNISH.

Take of virgin wax and gum asphaltum each 2 oz; of black pitch and Burgundy pitch each ½ oz; melt the wax and pitch in a new earthenware, glazed pot, and add to them, by degrees, the asphaltum, finely powdered. Let the whole boil, simmering gradually, till such time, as on taking a drop upon a plate it will break, when it is cold, on bending it double two or three times betwixt the fingers. The varnish being then boiled enough, must be taken off the fire, and, after it cools a little, must be poured into warm water, that it may work the more easily with the hands, so as to be formed into balls, which must be kneaded and put into a piece of taffety for use.

Painting and Gilding on Silk.

Having with the pounce bag and a pricked pattern transferred the lettering or design upon the silk, go over them first with a coat of japan varnish, (this will not spread on the silk,) and a clean, sharp edge can be made with it; upon this, when dry, work your colors.

For gold letters, size upon the japan surface with oil size, use the tip and cushion for laying the gold and rub the letters smooth with fine cotton wool. Shade with japan varnish first, following with the shading color as before; high lights must be added to complete the letter.

Japan Tin Signs.

These are a very neat and popular style of sign, but there are some difficulties attending a proper execution of them, that every painter may not be prepared to remedy.

Owing to imperfect baking, the japan on some tins is softer than others; this is more commonly the case with colored tins, making it difficult to accomplish a sharp, clean job, which is essential in work of this kind.

The following method will be found to work well. After cleaning your tin well with soft cotton, lay on your pattern and pounce it or if only one sign is to be done, this mode may be too tedious; lay it off with chalk crayon, dust it off with a badger or camel hair blender, and it will be ready for sizing.

For Size, mix 2 ounces coach body varnish and 2 ounces of medium or hard drying varnish, adding ¼ ounce of fat oil, into which sufficient yellow has been ground to give it a body; use oil of turpentine to reduce to a proper working consistency.

This will be ready to gild in from ten to twelve hours, use the tip and cushion in laying the leaf. Avoid touching with the finger.

After gilding, rub with cotton; the chalk marks will disappear and the tin will be quite clean.

Solution for Silvering Glass.

Prepare a mixture of 3 grs. of ammonia, 60 grs. nitrate of silver, 90 minims of water; when the nitrate of silver is dissolved, filter the liquid, and add 15 grs. sugar, dissolved in 1½ oz. of water and 1½ oz. spirits of wine. Coat all of the glass, with the exception of the part that is to be silvered with varnish; place it in the mixture, and let it remain a few days. It will be most beautifully silvered yet this method is far too expensive for ordinary work.

Another method of *gilding* on glass is by forming an amalgam of gold as follows: Throw into mercury as much gold leaf or foil as it will dissolve, stirring the amalgam after each addition. This must be preserved in a vial for future use.

The glass must be thoroughly cleaned and polished as usual, and then the amalgam is smeared over the part intended to be gilded.

The mercury is finally driven off by the application of heat, and the gold is left on the surface. The operation may be repeated again if the first coating is not sufficiently thick.

Glass and Porcelain Gilding.

Dissolve in boiled linseed oil an equal weight either of copal or amber; add as much oil of turpentine as will enable you to apply the compound or size thus formed, as thin as possible to the parts of the glass intended to be gilded.

The glass is to be placed in a stove till it will almost burn the fingers when handled; at this temperature, the size becomes adhesive, and gold leaf applied the usual way will immediately stick. Sweep off the superfluous portions of the leaf, and when cold it may be burnished, taking care to interpose a piece of India paper between the gold and the burnisher.

Another Method of Gilding China and Glass.

Powdered gold, is mixed with borax and gum water, and the solution applied with a camel hair pencil. Heat is then applied until the borax fuses, when the gold is fixed and may be burnished.

ENAMEL NUMBERS.

A beautiful enamel number, for hotels, dwellings, steamboats, church-pews; &c., is made by taking a large sized common watch crystal (they can be had by the quantity very cheap), painting or gilding a number upon the hollow side, and coating over with white, blue, or any color desired; it is afterwards filled up level with plaster of Paris; the plaster itself forms a beautiful white background. They are easily fastened to any surface with a cement made of white lead and Japan varnish or drier, mixed quite thick.

ENAMELED GLASS.

A very good imitation of figured or enameled glass is made by the following method: take French zine white, dry, and grind very fine with clear soft water; dissolve gum Arabic in water and put sufficient in the white to prevent it rubbing off when applied to the glass; thin it as much as necessary with water. Clean your glass well and with a wide camel hair varnish brush give it a coat of the white, blending it out even and smooth while wet, with a badger hair blender.

A stencil pattern must now be cut of the figure or design intended; for this use thick pattern paper, which has previously been well oiled with boiled linseed oil. This, when dry, makes the paper tough. Lay the stencil upon the white surface, and with a new scrubbing brush, brush out all the openings, leaving the figure or ornament clear and perfect upon the glass.

A coat of demar varnish completes the process, and renders the imitation perfect. When the glass is to be totally obscured, give the opposite side a coat of the white and also of the varnish.

WINDOW SHADE PAINTING.

Glue your muslin to the frame or stretcher; let it stand until dry, then open out as wide as it will allow and give a coat of glue size. Stretch while wet as tight as possible.

When the size is dry, coat with any color desired, both sides, mixing your color with benzine and Japan; when this is dry it is ready for the border and lettering; use varnish size, and gild with Florence leaf. Go over it afterwards with gold lacquer; it may then be cut from the frame and trimmed.

MAKING SIGN BOARDS, &c.

The best and most durable sign boards are made of white pine wood which has been perfectly seasoned. Poplar or white wood makes a smooth, nice surface to work upon, but will warp and twist on exposure to the weather. For signs at a distance from the ground canvas is sometimes substituted. It looks equally as well, and if well painted on both sides, will last a long time.

Sheet zinc is also used in imitation of board signs. It is much lighter, and dispenses with joints, which in boards are always liable to open. When more than one sheet is necessary, the edges can be butted together and soldered on the back, showing a perfectly smooth surface in front.

Zinc is also extensively used for circular corner signs, and for window sills, &c. A wooden frame is first made and fitted neatly to the place, and the zinc nailed to it previous to being painted.

Canvas or flag signs should be made of medium or light duck, and well bound with rope. Without this, the action of the weather will soon reduce them to ribbons. If openings are cut to admit the wind, they must also be well bound with canvas. Iron rings must be used for eyelets. They should be wired to the pole with copper wire.

SHOW CARD WRITING.

This has of late become quite an important business, and is often carried on in connection with Sign Painting. The mode of writing is, however, very different. A skillful card writer will astonish most sign painters with the rapidity of his movements; but neatness or precision is not always characteristic of their work. This is attributable, however, in a great degree, to their cheapness, and to the fact that they are generally intended to answer only a temporary purpose.

Show cards are of two classes—the plain or white and the colored.

On the former, the color of the letters are generally black; they are outlined with a solution of India ink and water, strong enough to leave a jet black mark. After outlining, they are filled in with turpentine asphaltum varnish, which dries in a few minutes and forms a beautiful black, glossy surface. The card selected for this purpose should have an enamel surface. When the letters are completed, with an ordinary pen, dipped in India ink, draw a line around the card, about one inch from the edge. This gives it a finished appearance and adds much to its attractiveness.

Colored cards afford a much larger scope for a display of taste than the plain. They can be had of almost every hue, and where a little judgment is exercised in the arrangement of the letters, colors, etc., they unquestionably form a very attractive sign. They are generally lettered with white.

For this purpose, take the best dry French zinc, grind well on a slab or in a mill, with just sufficient water to saturate it. After this is done, dissolve gum Arabic in water, and add to the white enough of the solution to prevent its rubbing off after being applied to the card. It will have to be tested until a proper consistency is arrived at. If it is too weak, it will rub off; if too strong, it will be liable to crack and chip off.

With this white, the letters are outlined, and when dry, filled in. It is necessary, in order to have a smooth, even surface, to flow as much of the white as will remain on the letter, leaving the card in a flat position until dry.

The colors used for shading are vermilion, Venetian red chrome green, ultramarine blue, chrome yellow, yellow ochre, burnt umber and burnt sienna; all of which must be dry, and treated in the same manner as the white. To lighten them to any required shade they must be mixed with the white.

It were useless to attempt to confine the writer to any one or half-dozen styles of shades, where such a free field for variety is offered. It is sufficient to say that every style of shade of which we have yet had occasion to speak, may be here reproduced, and fancy may have full scope.

In the colored cards, the marginal line must be made in white, which should be of such a consistency as to flow freely from the pen. As cards have, in numerous instances, to be mounted on frames or stretchers, we will describe the process for the benefit of those of our readers who may have such work to do.

Lay the stretcher on the card—which should be a little the largest—with a wet sponge dampen the surface, of the card inside the stretcher; have the glue hot; with a brush spread it quickly, but carefully, on the frame covering about an inch of the surface close to the edge all round; then carefully lay the glued side down on the card, press lightly on it, and turn the card uppermost, and with a clean cloth rub the edge of the card down close to the frame; place it between two flat surfaces, under weights, for a short time. When dry, it will be tight as a drum. The surplus edges of the card may then be trimmed off, and it is ready for lettering.

Lettering on Muslin, Transparencies, etc.

Much trouble is often caused, in this class of work by the oil or color spreading on all sides of the letter, giving it a blotted and blurred appearance. Wetting the muslin with water is generally resorted to obviate the difficulty.

By mixing the color entirely with benzine and benzine Japan the wetting process may be dispensed with, and a smooth clean job can be made.

Paper Patterns.

The heavy brown pattern paper is best for making pricked patterns. In case a pattern should be worn out or lost, it will be found convenient to have a duplicate. This may be made by pricking through two sheets at the same time. A pentagraph wheel will be of great assistance in making these patterns.

Pounce Ball or Bag

Is made by tying a quantity of dry white lead or Spanish whiting in two thicknesses of fine muslin. It is used to transfer letters, designs, &c., by means of pricked patterns, to signs and other surfaces, preparatory to painting or gilding. The punctured parts are dusted over with the bag, and on removing the paper, the design will be distinctly seen in small white dots upon the surface.

A dark pounce bag, for transferring to light surfaces, may be made by using dry Indian or Venetian red, in place of whiting.

INSURANCE SIGNS.

Sizing, by stencil patterns, will greatly facilitate work. When a large number of gold signs of the same patterns are to be made, as is often the case with insurance work, heavy paper stencils are generally used.

WHITE LEAD PUTTY

Is the best for filling sign boards, and for every description of sign work. The ordinary thick white lead in oil will answer, with a little Japan added, and worked to a proper consistency with whiting.

MAGIC TRACING PAPER.

This is made by mixing lamp black, or any other color, with sweet oil, and applying it with a brush or sponge to both sides of printers' book paper, afterwards rubbing well with a soft rag until no more color will come out.

By laying a sheet of this paper between a clean sheet and the design or drawing, and tracing the latter with a pointed stick or pencil, a distinct copy will be found on the lower sheet. It is valuable to sign painters for transferring purposes.

TRANSPARENT TRACING PAPER

For copying designs, drawings, &c., is made by mixing together at a gentle heat, one oz. of Canada balsam and a quarter pint spirits of turpentine; with a soft brush, spread it thinly over one side of good tissue paper. It dries quickly, is very transparent, and is not greasy, therefore does not stain the object upon which it may be placed.

PREPARED LAMP BLACK.

Ordinary lamp black before being used for sign or ornamental purposes, should be placed in a flat, sheet iron pan, and held over a hot fire until it ceases to smoke. By this method, it is divested of its greasy, non-drying qualities, and will then answer all the purposes of a vegetable black.

SAVING WASTE GOLD LEAF.

In the process of glass gilding, about two-thirds is superfluous or waste gold; this may be recovered by saving the cotton with which the glass has been cleaned. When a quantity is collected it may be burned in a crucible, and the gold recovered by means of lead; or the gold-beater will take the cotton and allow full value for the button obtained.

REMOVING FLOCK AND SMALT FROM OLD SIGN BOARDS.

Flock may generally be removed by the use of a steel scraper and coarse sand-paper.

Smalt often becomes so hard as to resist all efforts of this kind. A strong solution of concentrated lye should be made and applied to the surface of the board, repeating the application until it can be easily scraped off. The board should then be well washed with water, going over it afterwards, and previous to painting with strong vinegar. This neutralizes the alkali and prevents any injurious results to the paint.

Lettering Transparencies.

Stretch the muslin as tightly as possible upon the frame; with a brush give a coat of ordinary starch, of the consistency used for laundry purposes. When this is dry, the cloth will be quite tight, and will be found very easy to letter upon.

Smalts.

Smalts of various colors are made of fine lake sand, which must be free of dirt and well dried.

Mix the color, or paint for coloring purposes, with equal parts of oil and turpentine, adding a little Japan mix this with as much of the sand as it will color, rubbing it between the hands until quite loose and dry, then spread in the sun, or in a warm place, breaking up the lumps occasionally, and sifting as fast as dry through a fine sieve.

To every ten pounds of smalt add two ounces of frosting, which must be pounded fine and sifted into the smalt. After mixing thoroughly it is ready for use, and should be kept dry.

Frosting for Show Cards, Signs, etc.

Frosting is a thin, glassy substance, of various colors, use by painters and writers of show cards for sprinkling the surfaces of letters and giving them that beautiful crystalline appearance which is so much admired. It may also be used with beautiful effect for ground works. It is first put into a cloth and pounded fine, and then sifted upon the letters or surface while the paint is wet.

It is also used to give brilliancy to smalts, mixing in the proportion of two ounces of frosting to every ten or fifteen pounds of smalt.

TO PREVENT COLOR CRAWLING.

When a sign or other surface has been coated some time previous to lettering it is frequently difficult to apply the lettering color, on account of a disposition to creep or crawl, as on a greasy surface, to the great annoyance of the letterer. This will be remedied by previously rubbing with a cloth dampened with benzine, alcohol or water.

SILVER LEAF.

Silver leaf should be well varnished before being exposed to the weather. By applying a coat of gold lacquer, it can scarcely be detected from gold. On flocked or smalted signs the lacquer and varnish must be applied previous to cutting in.

TUBE COLORS.

Are the most convenient for ornamental glass work and all the finer branches of sign painting, but are too expensive for large surfaces or backgrounds.

SHELLAC VARNISH OR KNOTTING.

This is used for killing knots and gum spots on new pine boards, previous to painting. It is made in the following manner: Best alcohol, 1 gallon; nice gum shellac, 2½ pounds. Place the Jug or bottle in a situation to keep it just a little warm, and it will dissolve quicker than if hot, or left cold. When a very nice surface is required, the entire sign board may be coated with the varnish, adding for this purpose a little more alcohol.

IMPRESSIONS FROM PRINTS.

The print is soaked first in a solution of potash and then in one of tartaric acid. This produces a perfect solution of crystals in bi-tartarate of potash through the texture of the unprinted paper. As this salt repels the oil the ink roller may now be passed over the surface without transferring any of its contents to the paper, except in those parts to which the ink had been originally applied. The ink of the print prevents the saline matter from penetrating wherever it is present, and wherever there is no saline matter present the ink adheres; so that many impressions may be taken as in lithography.

MAPS AND CHARTS.

Maps, charts or engravings may be effectually varnished by running a very delicate coating of gutta-percha solution over their surface. It is perfectly transparent and will greatly improve the appearance of the picture.

<h1 style="text-align:center">MISCELLANEOUS RECEIPTS</h1>

Cobalt Smalt.—Roast cobalt ore to drive off the arsenic; make the residuum into a paste with oil of vitriol, and heat it to redness for an hour; powder dissolve in water, and precipitate the oxide of iron by carbonate of potash, gradually added until a rose-colored powder begins to fall; then decant the clear, and precipitate by a solution of silicate of potash prepared by fusing together for five hours a mixture of 10 parts of potash, 15 parts of finely-ground flints, and 1 part charcoal. The precipitate, when dry, may be fused and powdered very fine.

Glass Staining.—The following colors, after having been prepared, and rubbed upon a plate of ground glass, with the spirit of turpentine or lavender, thickened in the air, are applied with a hair-pencil. Before using them, however, it is necessary to try them on small pieces of glass, and expose them to the fire, to ascertain if the desired tone of color is produced. The artist must be guided by these proof-pieces in using his colors. The glass, proper for receiving these pigments should be colorless, uniform, and difficult of fusion. A design must be drawn on paper, and placed beneath the plate of glass. The upper side of the glass, being sponged over with gum-water, affords, when dry, a surface proper for receiving the colors without the risk of their running irregularly, as they would otherwise do on the slippery glass. The artist draws on the plate (usually in black), with a fine pencil, all the traces which mark the great outlines or shades of the figure. Afterwards, when it is dry, the vitrifying colors are laid on by means of a larger hair pencil; their selection being regulated by the burnt specimen-tints above mentioned. The following are all fast colors, which do not run, except the yellow, which must, therefore, be laid on the opposite side of the glass. The preparations being all laid on, the glass is ready for being fired in a muffle, in order to fix and bring out the proper colors. The muffle must be made of very refractory fire-clay, flat at its bottom, and only five or six inches high, with a strong arched roof, and close on all sides, to exclude smoke and flame. On the bottom, a smooth bed of sifted lime, freed from water, about half an inch thick, must be prepared for receiving the glass. Sometimes, several plates of glass are laid over each other, with a layer of lime powder between each. The fire is now lighted, and very gradually raised, lest the glass should be broken; then keep it at a full heat for three or four hours, more or less, according to the indications of the trial slips; the yellow color being principally watched, it furnishing the best criterion of the state of the others. When all is right, let the fire die out, so as to anneal the glass.

Stained Glass Pigments—No. 1. *Flesh-color.*—Red-lead, 1 oz.; red-enamel (Venetian glass enamel, from alum and copperas calcined together;) grind them to a fine powder, and work this up with alcohol upon a hard stone. When slightly baked, this produces a fine flesh color. No. 2. *Black Color*—Take 14½ oz. of smithy scales of iron; mix them with two oz. white glass; antimony, 1 oz.; manganese, ½ oz.; pound and grind these ingredients together, with strong vinegar. No. 3. *Brown Color.*—White glass or enamel, 1 oz,; good manganese, ½ oz.; grind together. No. 4. *Red, Rose and Brown Colors* are made from peroxide of iron, prepared by nitric acid. The flux consists of borax, sand, and minium, in small quantities. *Red Color* may likewise be obtained from 1 oz. of red chalk, pounded, mixed with 2 oz. of white, hard enamel, and a little peroxide of copper. *A Red* may also be composed of rust of iron, glass of antimony, yellow glass of lead, such as is used by potters (or litharge), each in equal quantities; to which a little sulphuret of silver is added. This composition, well ground, produces a very fine red color-on glass. No. 5. *Green.*—2 oz. of brass, calcined into an oxide; 2 oz. of minium and 8 oz. white sand: reduce them to a fine powder, which is to be enclosed in a well-luted crucible, and heated strongly in an air-furnace for an hour. When the mixture is cold, grind it in a brass mortar. Green may, however, be advantageously produced, by a yellow on one side, and a blue on the other. Oxide of chrome has been also employed to stain glass green. No. 6. *A Fine Yellow Stain*—Take fine silver, laminated thin, dissolve in nitric acid, dilute with abundance of water, and precipitate with solution of sea-salt; mix this chloride of silver in a dry powder, with three times its weight of pipe-clay, well burnt and powdered. The back of the glass pane is to be painted with this powder: for, when painted on the face, it is apt to run into the colors. *A Pale Yellow* can be made by mixing sulphuret of silver with glass of antimony and yellow ochre, previously calcined to a red-brown tint. Work all these powders together, and paint on the back of the glass. Oxide silver *laminæ*, melted with sulphur, and glass of antimony, thrown into cold water, and afterwards ground to a powder, afford a yellow. *A Pale Yellow* may be made with the powder resulting from brass, sulphur, and glass of antimony, calcined together in a crucible till they cease to smoke, and then mixed with a little burnt yellow-ochre. *The Fine Yellow* of M. Meraud is prepared from chloride of silver, oxide of zinc, and rust of iron. This mixture, simply ground, is applied on the glass. *Orange Color.*—Take 1 part of silver powder, as precipitated from the nitrate of that metal, by plates of copper, and washed: mix with 1 part of red ochre, and 1 of yellow, by careful trituration; grind into a thin paste, with oil of turpentine or lavender; apply this with a brush and burn in.

Porcelain Colors.—The following are some of the colors used in the celebrated porcelain manufactory of Sevres, and the proportions in which they are compounded. Though intended for porcelain painting, nearly all are applicable to painting on glass. Flux No. 1 minium or red lead, 3 parts; white sand, washed, 1 part. This mixture is melted, by which it is converted into a greenish-colored glass. Flux No. 2. *Gray Flux.*—Of No. 1, 8 parts; fused borax in powder, 1 part. This mixture is melted. Flux No. 3. *For Carmines and Greens.*—Melt together fused borax, 5 parts calcined flint, 3 parts; pure minium, 1 part. No. 1. *Indigo Blue.*—Oxide of cobalt, 1 part; flux No.3, 2 parts. *Deep Azure Blue.*—Oxide of cobalt, 1 part oxide of zinc, 2 parts; flux No. 3, 5 parts. No. 2. *Emerald Green.*—Oxide of copper 1 part: antimonic acid, 10 parts; flux No. 1, 30 parts. Pulverize together, and melt. No. 3. *Grass Green.*—Green oxide of chromium, 1 part; flux No, 3, 3 parts. Triturate and melt. No. 4, *Yellow.*—Antimonic acid, 1 part; subsulphate of the peroxide of iron, 8 parts; oxide of zinc, 4 parts; flux No. 1, 36 parts. Rub up together and melt. If this color is too deep, the salt of iron is diminished. No. 5. *Fixed Yellow, for touches.*—No. 4, 1 part; White enamel of commerce, 2 parts. Melt and pour out; if not sufficiently fixed, a little sand may be added. No. 6. *Deep Nankin Yellow.*—Subsulphate of iron, 1 part; oxide of zinc, 2 parts; flux No. 2. 8 parts. Triturate without melting. No. 7. *Deep Red.*—Subsulphate of iron, calcined in a muffle until it becomes of a beautiful capucine red, 1 part; flux No. parts; mix without melting. No. 8. *Liver Brown.*—Oxide of iron made of a red brown, and mixed with three times its weight of flux No.2. A tenth of sienna earth is added to it, if it is not deep enough. No. 9. *White.*—The white enamel of commerce in cakes. No. 10. *Deep Blade.*—Oxide of cobalt, 2 parts; copper, 2 parts; oxide of manganese. 1 part; flux No. 1, 6 parts; fused borax ½ part. Melt and add oxide of manganese, 1 part; oxide of copper, 2 parts. Triturate without melting.

The Application.—Follow the general directions given in another part of this work, in relation to staining glass.

Soluble Glass.—1. Silica, 1 part; carbonate of soda, 2 parts; fuse together. 2. Carbonate of soda (dry). 54 parts; dry carbonate of potassa, 70 parts; silica, 192 parts; soluble in boiling water, yielding a fine transparent, semi elastic varnish. 3. Carbonate of potassa (dry), 10 parts; powdered quartz (or sand free from iron or alumina), 15 parts; charcoal, 1 part; all fused together. Soluble in 5 or 6 times its weight of boiling water. The filtered solution evaporated to dryness yields a transparent glass, permanent in the air.

To Drill and Ornament Glass.—Glass can be easily drilled with a steel drill, hardened but not drawn, and driven at a high velocity. Holes of any size, from the 16th of an inch upwards, can be drilled, by using spirits of turpentine as a dip; and, easier still, by using camphor with the turpentine. Do not press the glass very hard against the drill. If you require to ornament glass by turning in a lathe, use a good mill file and the turpentine and camphor dip, and you will find it an easy matter to produce any shape you choose.

To Make Door Plater.— Cut your glass the right size, and make it perfectly clean with alcohol or soap; then cut a strip of tin-foil sufficiently long and wide for the name, and with a piece of ivory or other burnisher rub it lengthwise to make it smooth; now wet the glass with the tongue (as saliva is the best sticking substance), or if the glass is very large, use a weak solution of gum arabic, or the white of an egg in half a pint of water, and lay on the foil, rubbing it down to the glass with a bit of cloth, then also with the burnisher; the more it is burnished the better will it look; now mark the width of the foil which is to be the height of the letter, and put on a straight edge, and hold it firmly to the foil, and with a sharp knife cut the foil, and take off the superfluous edges; then either lay out the letters on the back of the foil (so they shall read correctly on the front) by your own judgment or by means of pattern letters, which can be purchased for that purpose; cut with the knife, carefully holding down the pattern or straight edge, whichever you use; then rub down the edge of all the letters with the back of the knife, or edge of the burnisher, which prevents the black paint or japan which you next put over the back of the plate, from getting under the foil; having put a line above and one below the name, or a border around the whole plate or not, as you bargain for the job. The japan is made by dissolving asphaltum in just enough turpentine to cut it; apply with a brush, as other paint, over the back of the letters, and over the glass forming a background. This is used on the iron plate of the frame also, putting it on when the plate is a little hot; and, as soon as it cools, it is dry. A little lamp-black may be rubbed into it if you desire it any blacker than it is without it.

To Transfer Prints. Etc. to Glass.—Take of gum sandarach, 4 oz; mastic, 1 oz.; Venice turpentine, 1 oz.; alcohol, 15 oz. Digest in a bottle, frequently shaking, and it is ready for use. Directions: use, if possible, good plate glass of the size of the picture to be transfered, go over it with the above varnish, beginning at one side, press down the picture firmly and evenly as you proceed, so that no air can possibly lodge between; put aside, and let it dry perfectly, then moisten the paper cautiously with water, and remove it piece-meal by rubbing carefully with the fingers; if managed nicely, a complete transfer of the picture to the glass will be effected.

To Make Paper into Parchment.—To produce this transformation, take unsized paper and plunge it into a solution of two parts of concentrated sulphuric acid combined with 1 part water; withdraw it immediately, and wash it in clean water, and the change is complete. It is now fit for writing; for the acid supplies the want of size, and it becomes so strong that a strip 2 or 3 inches wide will bear from 60 to 80 lbs. weight, while a like strip of parchment will bear only about 25 lbs.

Gilding Glass Signs, Etc.—Cut a piece of thin paper to the size of your glass, draw out your design correctly in black lead-pencil on paper, then prick through the outline of the letters with a fine needle, tie up a little dry white lead in a piece of rag; this is a pounce-bag. Place your design upon the glass, right side up, dust it with the pounce-bag; and, after taking the paper off, the design will appear in white dots upon the glass; these will guide you in laying on the gold on the opposite side, which must be *well cleaned* preparatory to laying on the gold. *Preparing the Size.* Boil perfectly clean water in an enameled sauce-pan, and while boiling, add 2 or three shreds of best selected is in glass, after a few minutes strain it through a clean linen rag; when cool it is ready for use. *Clean the Glass Perfectly.*—When this is done, use a flat camel's-hair brush for laying on the size; and let it drain off when you put the gold on. When the gold is laid on and perfectly dry, take a ball of the finest cotton wool and gently or polish the gold, you can then lay on another coat of gold if desirable, it is now ready for writing. In doing this mix a little of the best vegetable black with black japan; thin with turpentine to a proper working consistency; apply this, when thoroughly dry; wash off the superfluous gold, and shade as in sign-writing.

Gilders' Gold Size.—Drying or boiled linseed oil, thickened with yellow ochre, or calcined red ochre, and carefully reduced to the utmost smoothness by grinding. It is thinned with oil of turpentine.

To Gild Letters on Wood, Etc.—When your sign is prepared as smooth as possible, go over it with a sizing made by the white of an egg dissolved in about four times its weight of cold water; adding a small quantity of fuller's earth, this is to prevent the gold sticking to any part but the letters. When dry lay out the letter and commence writing, laying on the size as thinly as possible, with a sable pencil. Let it stand until you can barely feel a slight stickiness, then go to work with your gold-leaf, knife and cushion, and gild the letters. Take a leaf up on the point of your knife, after giving it a slight puff into the back part of your cushion, and spread it on the front part of the cushion as straight as possible, giving it another slight puff with your mouth to flatten it out. Now cut it into the proper size, cutting with the heel of your knife forwards. Now rub the tip lightly on your hair; take up the gold on the point, and place it neatly on the letters: when they are all covered get some very fine cotton wool, and gently rub the gold until it is smooth and bright. Then wash the sign with clean water to take off the egg size.

French Burnished Gilding.—*Encollage*, or Glue Coat.—To a decoction of wormwood and garlic in water, strained through a cloth, a little common salt and some vinegar are added. This is mixed with as much good glue, and the mixture spread in a hot state with a brush of boar's hair. When plaster or marble is gilded, leave out the salt. The first glue coating is made thinner than the second. 2. *White preparation* consists in covering the above surface with 8, 10 or 12 coats of Spanish white, mixed up with strong size; each well worked on with the brush. 3. *Stop* up the pores with thick whiting and glue, and smooth the surface with dog-skin. 4. *Polish* the surface with pumice stone and very cold water. 5. *Retouch* the whole in a skillful manner. 6. *Cleanse* with a damp linen rag, and then a soft sponge. 7. *Rub* with a horse's tail (*shave grass*) the parts to be yellowed, to make them softer. 8. *Yellow* with *yellow ochre* carefully ground in water, and mixed with transparent colorless size. Use the thinner part of the mixture with a fine brush. 9. Next rub the work with shave grass to remove any granular appearance. 10. *Gold water size* consists of Armenian bowl, 1 lb.; bloodstone [hematite], 2 oz.; and as much galena, each separately ground in water. Then mix all together with a spoonful of olive oil. This is tempered with a white sheep skin glue, clear and well strained. Heat and apply three coats with a fine long -haired brush. *Rub* with a clean, dry, linen cloth, except the parts to be burnished, which are to receive other two coats of the gold size, tempered with glue. 12. The surface, damped with cold water (iced in summer), has then the *gold-leaf* applied to it. Gild the *hollow* ground before the more prominent parts; water being dexterously applied by a soft brush, immediately behind the gold leaf, before laying it down; removing any excess of water with a dry brush. 13. *Burnish* with bloodstone. 14. Next pass a thin coat of glue, slightly warmed, over the parts that are not to be burnished. 15. Next moisten any broken points with a brush, and apply bits of gold leaf to them. 16. Apply the *vermeil* coat very lightly over the gold-leaf with a soft brush. It gives lustre and fire to the gold, and is made as follows, annotto, 2 oz.; gamboge, 1 oz.; vermilion 1 oz.; dragon's-blood, ½ oz.; salt of tartar, 2 oz., saffron, 18 grs.; boil in 2 English pints of water, over a slow fire, till it is reduced to a fourth; then pass the whole through silk or muslin sieve. 17. Next pass over the dead surfaces a second coat of deadening glue, hotter than the first. This finishes the work, and gives it strength.

Gliding on Wood.—To gild in oil, the wood, after being properly smoothed, is covered with a coat of *gold size*, made of drying linseed oil mixed with yellow ochre; when this has become so dry as to adhere to the fingers without soiling them, the gold leaf is laid on with great care and dexterity, and pressed down with cotton wool; places that have been missed are covered with small pieces of gold leaf, and when the whole is dry, the ragged bits are rubbed off with the cotton. This is by far the easiest mode of gilding; Any other metallic leaves may be applied in a similar manner. *Pale leaf gold* has a greenish yellow color, and is an alloy of gold with silver. Dutch gold leaf is only copper leaf colored with fumes of zinc; being much cheaper than true gold leaf, it is very useful when large quantities of gilding is required in places where it can be defended from the weather, as it changes color if exposed to moisture; and it should be covered with varnish. *Silver leaf* is prepared every way the same as gold leaf; but when applied should be kept well covered with varnish, otherwise it is liable to tarnish; a transparent yellow varnish will give it the appearance of gold. Whenever gold is fixed by means of linseed oil, it will bear washing off, which burnished gold will not.

True Gold Powder.—Put some gold leaf, with a little honey, or thick gum water made with gum-arabic, into an earthen mortar, and pound the mixture till the gold is reduced to very small particles then wash out the honey or gum repeatedly with warm water, and the gold in powder will be left behind. When dry, it is fit for use.

Dutch Gold Powder is made from Dutch gold-leaf, which is sold in books at a very low price. Treat in the manner described above for true gold-powder. When this inferior powder is used, cover the gilding with a coat of clear varnish, otherwise it will soon lose its bright appearance.

Magic Paper—Take lard oil or sweet oil, mixed to the consistency of cream, with either of the following paints, the color of which is desired: Prussian blue, lamp-black, Venetian red, or chrome green, either of which should be rubbed with a knife on a plate or stone until smooth. Use rather thin but firm paper; put on with a sponge, and wipe off as dry as convenient; then lay them between uncolored paper, or between newspapers, and press by laying books or some other flat substances upon them until the surplus oil is absorbed, when it is ready for use.

Flexible Paint for Canvas.—Yellow soap 2½ lbs., boiling water 1½ gallons, dissolve; grind the solution while hot with *good oil paint,* 1¼ cwt. Use for canvas.

Painter's Cream.—Pale nut oil 6 ozs., mastic 1 oz., dissolve; add of sugar of lead ¼ oz., previously ground in the least possible quantity of oil, then add of water *q. s.*, gradually, until it acquires the consistency of cream, working it well all the time. Used to cover the unfinished work of painters. It will wash off with water.

Gold Lacquer.—Put into a clean four-gallon tin one pound of ground turmeric, one and a half ounces of gamboge, three and a half pounds of powdered gum sandarach, three-quarters of a pound of shellac, and two gallons of spirits of wine. When shaken, dissolved, and strained, add one pint of turpentine varnish, well mixed.

Gold Varnish.—Digest shellac, sixteen parts gum sandarach, mastic of each three parts; crocus, one part; gum gamboge, two parts; all bruised, with alcohol, one hundred and forty-four parts. Or, digest seedlac, sandarach mastic, of each eight parts; gamboge, two parts; dragon's-blood one part; white turpentine, six parts; turmeric, four parts; bruised with alcohol, one hundred and twenty parts.

Deep Gold Colored Lacquer.—Seedlac, three ounces; turmeric, one ounce dragon's-blood, one-fourth ounce; alcohol, one pint; digest for a week, frequently shaking; decant and filter.

To Silver Ivory.—Pound a small piece of nitrate of silver in a mortar, add soft water to it, mix them well together, and keep in a vial for use. When you wish to silver any article immerse it in this solution, let it remain till it turns of a deep yellow; then place it in clear water and expose it to the rays of the sun. If you wish to depicture a figure, name, or cypher, on your ivory, dip a camel's-hair pencil in the solution, and draw the subject on the ivory. After it has turned a deep yellow, wash it well with water, and place it in the sunshine, occasionally wetting it with pure water. In a short time it will turn of a deep black color, which, if well rubbed, will change to a brilliant silver.

To Gild Ivory.—Immerse it in a solution of nitro muriate of gold, and then expose it to hydrogen gas while damp. Wash it afterwards in clean water.

Varnish for Frames, Etc.—Lay the frames over with tin or silver foil by means of plaster of Paris, glue, or cement of some kind, that the foil may be perfectly adherent to the wood; then apply your gold lacquer varnish, which is made as follows: Ground tumeric, 1 lb.; powdered gamboge, 1½ ounces; powdered sandarach, 3½ lbs.; powdered shellac, ¾ lb.; spirits of wine, 2 gals; dissolve and strain then add turpentine varnish, 1 pint; and it is ready for use.

Reviver for Gilt Frames.—White of eggs, 2 oz; chloride of potash or soda, 1 oz.; mix well, blow off the dust from the frames; then go over them with a soft brush dipped in the mixture, and they will appear equal to new.

Gilders' Pickle.—Alum and common salt, each 1 oz; nitre 2 oz; dissolve in water 5 pint. Used to impart a rich yellow color to gold surfaces. It is best used largely diluted with water.

To Make Letters or Flowers on Polished Steel.—Hold the steel over a charcoal fire till it becomes blue; let it cool. Then with equal parts of rosin and beeswax, melted together, colored a little with lamp-black, and diluted with spirits of turpentine, so as to work freely with a camel's -hair pencil, draw any letters or figures on the steel, while it is a little warm. When the steel has become cold, wash it over with muriatic acid; diluted with two parts to one of acid; you thus take off the blue color, and then wash it with clear water. Afterward, the varnish, being warmed a little, may be readily washed off with spirits of turpentine, and the letters or flowers will remain blue.

If letters are formed on polished steel with this varnish, and the body of the metal be also covered with it, except a small space round the letters, and then bathed with muriatic acid, the space round the letters will become a dull iron color, while the letters and the body of the steel will retain their polished surface and brilliancy.

To Silver Looking-Glasses.—Clean the glass plates by any of the methods adopted in gilding, as with alcohol and rotten-stone, and finally polish the surface with a buckskin buffer.

Now lay upon this surface a sheet of pure tin foil without flaw of any kind, and press out all the wrinkles so that it lies flat and even. A quantity of mercury is now poured upon the surface so as to cover it completely and uniformly.

Several folds of blotting paper are now placed upon the amalgam, and over these a board of the same size as the glass-plate is pressed into contact by means of weights on its upper surface. The pressure is maintained for some time. The excess of mercury is thus pressed out over the edges, and may be collected for the preparation of the next plate.

After the expiration of a number of days the pressure is removed, and the glass-plate is ready for use.

To Wash Iron or Steel with Gold.—Mix together in a vial one part of nitric acid with two parts of muriatic acid, and add as much fine gold as the acid will dissolve. For this purpose, gold-leaf is the most convenient, as it will be the most readily dissolved. (This solution is called the muriate of gold.) Pour over this solution, cautiously, about half as much sulphuric ether—shake the mixture, and then allow it to settle. The other will take the gold from the acid, and will separate itself from it also, and from an upper stratum in the vial. Carefully pour off this auriferous ether into another vial and cork it close. Wash any piece of steel or iron with this ether, and immediately plunge it in cold water, and it will have acquired a coat of pure gold. With this also any flowers or letters may be drawn or written even with a pen, and will appear perfectly gilt. The steel or iron should afterward be heated as much as it will bear without changing color, and if the steel be previously polished, the beauty of the gilding may be much increased by burnishing with a cornelian or blood-stone.

How to Write on Glass in the Sun.—Dissolve chalk in acquafortis to the consistency of milk, and add to that a strong dissolution of silver. Keep this in a glass decanter well stopped. Then cut out from a paper the letters you would have appear, and paste the paper on the decanter or jar, which you are to place in the sun in such a manner that its rays may pass through the spaces cut out of the paper, and fall on the surface of the liquor. The part of the glass through which the rays pass will turn black, whilst that under the paper will remain white. Do not shake the bottle during the operation. Used for lettering jars.

Jet or Polish for Wood or Leather, Black, Red, or Blue.—Alcohol [98 per cent], 1 pint; sealing wax, the color desired 3 sticks; dissolve by heat, and have it warm when applied. A sponge is the best to apply it with.

Japan Drier, Best Quality.—Take linseed oil one gallon; put into it gum shellac, ¾ lb.; litharge and burned Turkey umber, each ½ lb.; red lead ½ lb.; sugar of lead, 6 ounces. Boil in the oil till all are dissolved, which will require about four hours; remove from the fire, and stir in spirits of turpentine 1 gallon, and it is done.

Another—Linseed oil, 5 gallons; add red lead and letharge, each 3½ lbs.; raw umber, 1¼ lbs.; sugar of lead and sulphate of zinc, each ½ lb.; pulverize all the articles together, and boil in the oil till dissolved; when a little cool, thin with turpentine, 5 gallons.

Drying Oil Equal to Patent Driers at one-quarter their Price.—Linseed oil, 2 gallons; red lead and umber, each, 4 oz; sulphate of zinc, 2 oz.; sugar of lead, 2 oz. Boil until it will scorch a feather, when it is ready for use.

The Bronzing of Plaster Casts is effected by giving them a coat of oil or size varnish, and when this is nearly dry, applying with a dabber of cotton or camel-hair pencil any of the metallic bronze powders; or the powder may be placed in a little bag of muslin and dusted over the surface, and afterwards finished with a wad of linen. The surface must be afterwards varnished.

Polishes. 1. Carvers' Polish.—White resin, 2 oz; seedlac, 2 oz.; Spirits of wine, 1 pt. Dissolve. It should be laid on warm. Avoid moisture and dampness when used. 2. *French Polish.*—Gum shellac, 1 oz.; gum arabic, ¼ oz.; gum copal, ¼ oz. Powder and sift through a piece of muslin, put them in a closely corked bottle with 1 pint of spirits of wine, in a very warm situation, shaking every day till the gums are dissolved; then strain through muslin and cork for use. 3. *Polish for Dark Colored Woods.*—Seedlac, 1 oz.; Gum guaiacum, 2 drs.; dragon's-blood, 2 drs.; gum mastic, 2 drs.; put in a bottle with 1 pint of spirits of wine, cork close, expose to moderate heat till gums are dissolved strain into a bottle for use, with ¼ gill of linseed oil; shake together. 4. *Water-proof Polish.*—Gum henjam, 2 oz; gum sandarach 1 oz; gum anima, ¼ oz; spirits of wine, 1 pint. Mix in a closely stopped bottle, and place either in a sand bath or in hot water till the gums are dissolved, then strain off the mixture, shake it up with a ¼ gill of the best clear poppy oil and put it by for use. 5. *Finishing Polish.*—Gum shellac, 2 drs.; gum henjam, 2 drs.; put into ½ pint of best rectified spirits of wine in a bottle closely corked, keep in a warm place, shaking frequently until the gums are dissolved. When cold, shake up with it two tea-spoonfuls of the best clear poppy oil.

Mastic Varnish.—Mastic, 1 lb.; white wax, 1 oz; spirits turpentine, 1 gallon; reduce the gums small; then digest it with heat in a close vessel till dissolved.

Fictitious Linseed Oil.—Fish or vegetable oil, 100 gallons: acetate of lead, 7 lbs., letharge, 7 lbs.; dissolve in vinegar, 2 gallons. Well mixed with heat, then add boiled oil, 7 gallons; turpentine, 1 gallon. Again well mix.

Glazier's Putty:—Whiting, 70 lbs.; boiled oil, water two gallons. Mix; if too thin add more whiting; it too thick, add more oil.

Varnishes. Common Oil Varnish.—Resin, 4 lbs.; beeswax, ½ lb.; boiled oil, 1 gallon; mix with heat; then add spirits of turpentine, 2 quarts.

Beautiful Pale Amber Varnish.—Amber, pale and transparent, 6 lbs.; fuse; add hot clarified linseed oil, 2 gallons; boil till it strings strongly, cool a little, and add oil of turpentine 4 gals. This soon becomes very hard and is the most durable of oil varnishes. When wanted to dry quicker, drying oil may be substituted for linseed, or "driers" may be added during the cooling.

Body Varnish—Finest African copal, 8 lbs.; fuse carefully; add clarified oil, 2 gals boil gently for four and a-half hours, or until quite stringy; cool a little, and thin with oil of turpentine, 3 ½ gallons. Dries slowly.

Carriage Varnish.—Sandarach, 19 oz; Pale shellac, 9½ oz; very pale transparent resin, 12½ oz turpentine, 18 oz; 85 per cent. alcohol, 5 pts.: dissolve. Used for the internal parts of carriages, &c. Dries in ten minutes.

Compound Iron Paint.—Finely pulverized iron filings, 1 part; brick dust, 1 part; and ashes, 1 part. Pour over them glue water or size, set the whole near the fire, and, when warm, stir them well together. With this paint cover all the wood-work which may be in danger; when dry, give a second coat, and the wood will be rendered incombustible.

Best Wash for Barns and Houses.—Water lime, 1 pk.; freshly slacked lime, 1 pk.; yellow ochre in powder, 4 lbs.; burnt umber, 4 lbs. To be dissolved in hot water, and applied with a brush.

Durable Outside Paint.—Take 2 parts [in bulk] of water lime, ground fine; 1 part [in bulk] of white lead, in oil. Mix them thoroughly, by adding best boiled linseed oil, enough to prepare it to pass through a paint mill; after which, temper with oil till it can be applied with a common paint-brush. Make any color to suit. It will last three times as long as lead paint. IT IS SUPERIOR.

Farmers' Paint.—Farmers will find the following profitable for house or fence paint: Skim milk two quarts; fresh slacked lime, eight ounces; linseed oil, 6 ounces; white Bergundy pitch two ounces; Spanish White, three lbs. The lime is to be slacked in water exposed to the air, and then mixed with about one-fourth of the milk; the oil in which the pitch is dissolved to be added a little at a time; then the rest of the milk and afterwards the Spanish white. This is sufficient for twenty-seven yards, two coats. This is for white paint. If desirable, any other color may be produced thus, if a cream color is desired in place of part of the Spanish white, use the ochre alone.

Premium Paint without Oil or Lead.—Slack stonelime with boiling water in a tub or barrel to keep in the steam; then pass six quarts through a fine sieve. Now to this quantity add one quart of coarse salt, and 1 gallon of water; boil the mixture and skim it clear. To every 5 gallons of this skimmed mixture, add 1 lb. alum; ½ lb. coperas; and by slow degrees ¾ lb. potash, and 4 quarts sifted ashes or fine sand; add any coloring desired. A more durable paint was never made.

Green Paints for Garden Stands, Blinds, Etc.—Take mineral green, and white lead, ground in turpentine; mix up the quantity you wish with a small quantity of turpentine varnish. This serves for the first coat. For the second, put as much varnish in your mixture as will produce a good gloss. If you desire a brighter green, add a little Prussian blue, which will improve the color.

Milk Paint for Barns, any Color.—Mix water lime with skim-milk to a proper consistency to apply with a brush, and it is ready for use. It will adhere to wood, whether smooth or rough, to brick, mortar, or stone, where oil has not been used [in which case it leaves to some extent], and forms a very hard substance, as durable as the best oil paint. It is too cheap to estimate, and anyone can put it on who can use a brush. Any color may be given to it, by using colors of the tinge desired. If a red is preferred, mix Venetian-red with milk, not using any lime. It looks well for fifteen years.

www.ingramcontent.com/pod-product-compliance
Lightning Source LLC
Chambersburg PA
CBHW030830060726
47590CB00004B/1475